www.FlowerpotPress.com
PAB-0808-0182 · 978-1-4867-1513-8
Made in the U.S.A./Fabriqué aux États-Unis

FEET

Who has
HAPPY FEET
like these?

A penguin!

Who has
SCALY FEET
like this?

A crocodile!

Who has HOOFED FEET like these?

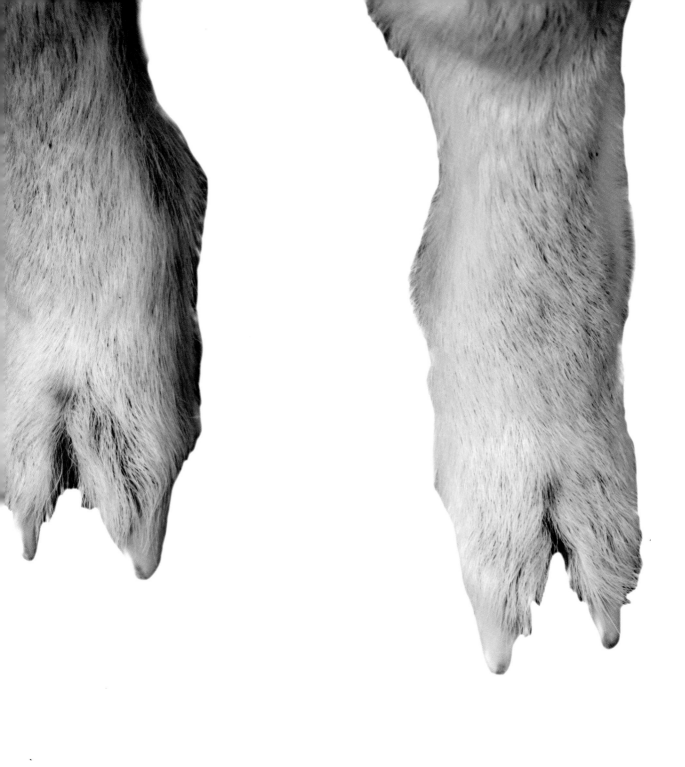

A goat!

Who has WEBBED FEET like these?

A duck!

Who has SPOTTED FEET like these?

A leopard!